BROKEN TIDE

BROKEN TIDE

EBI YEIBO

malthouse **МР**

Malthouse Press Limited

Lagos, Benin, Ibadan, Jos, Port-Harcourt, Zarla

© Ebi Yeibo 2023
First Published 2023
ISBN 978-978-59611-1-9

Published by Malthouse Press Limited

Lagos   Jos   Port Harcourt   Zaria

43 Onitana Street, Off Stadium Hotel Road,
Off Western Avenue, Lagos Mainland
E-mail: malthouselagos@gmail.comFacebook:@malthouselagos
Twitter:@malthouselagos Instagram:@malthouselagos
Tel: 0802 600 3203

International Distributors
African Books Collective, Oxford, UK Email:
abc@africanbookscollective.com
Website: http://www.africanbookscollective.com

DEDICATION

For
J. P. Clark-Bekederemo
Pathfinder
eternal songster....

ACKNOWLEDGEMENTS

I am eternally indebted to Friday Okon, for the Foreword; Egya Sule, Uche Nduka, Tade Ipadeola, for the blurbs; Ernest Brisibe, Angodi Agbor and Ebi Kedikumor, for the insights onIzon folklore and orthography. God bless you all exceedingly.

FOREWORD

Broken Tide is the voice of a master-craftsman whose message goes beyond the confines of his immediate environment to encompass Africa and the world. The collection is a kaleidoscope of images, memories and presages that take in their stride the present, the past and the future of the Niger Delta, Nigeria, Africa and the world. Foregrounded with the premonitions of Kadabramu (the poet's grandmother), the poems take a sardonic swipe at environmental issues (which is evident in the title of the collection), as well as political issues such as the minority/majority discourse, the politics of domination and exclusion, the politics of resource allocation and divide-and-rule tactics, underdevelopment of the Niger Delta, and the turgid corruption and leadership failure which have made the nation a bye-word in the comity of nations, among other issues. In fact, the issues interrogated in this collection are numerous, varied and nearly inexhaustible. The poet is another black *Orpheus*, on a quest or pilgrimage of sorts, in search of answers to the depredations visited on his people. Here is a troubadour whose love for his people and country is so overwhelming and powerful that his songs traverse the landscapes of rape, injustice, brutality, pain and dispossession visited by the leaders on the led.

Many of the poems are deep and allegorical, which on rereading, are amenable to different levels of meaning. One very outstanding quality of this collection is the overarching deployment of sound elements, especially alliterations and assonance, redolent of another past African/Nigerian master-craftsman, Okigbo. The collection pulsates with raw power and urgency, and the lilting mellifluous tenderness of a traditional African bard caught in the painful throes of love for his nation.

I recommend this collection to all Niger Deltans, Nigerians from all walks of life, all Africans at home and in the Diaspora, and all peoples of the developing nations who dream of throwing off the yoke of colonial and post-colonial bondage.

DR. FRIDAY OKON
University of Uyo, Nigeria

The numbers of midnight are reckoned.
- *Pablo Neruda*

The river sweats oil and tar...
- *T. S. Eliot*

The "Temple of Justice" is broken in every brick.
- *Niyi Osundare*

CONTENTS

THE POEMS

DARK SIGNS

Whenever a bird flies into the home

The signs are dark, or so,
Kadabramu* encored on her sick bed
Her voice barely audible
Sometimes, wheezing incoherent stuff.

Or a mahogany in the centre
Of River Forcados falls from the roots
Without whirlpool or wind
Or some wayward axe

Or the cracking sound of beings
Baling water from an unseen canoe
Ruffles the eerie silence
Of adjoining forests

Or *Gbele*** appears on the rack
The royal worm in the family hearth
Or one perceives the smell of ghosts
Crossing to *duamabou*...****

Nowadays, double-headed snakes
Cross the path of canoes
Stalling the journey at will
With their tangling strides

---

* Poet's maternal grandmother.
** A kind of wall gecko.
**** Land of ghosts.

Cocks crow their throats out
 In the neighbourhood
Full of hisses and kisses
Open covens, misty monasteries

Owls hoot day and night
And even beyond
Rolling distressed eyes
In impassioned prophecy

Fish jump into cruising canoes
Without prompting or warning
Or even a hint to unknot the clog
In the eye of the unblinking sun...

The signs are dark, or so,
Kadabramu encored on her sick bed
 Her voice barely audible
Sometimes, wheezing incoherent stuff.

HARPY BLOOD
For Oronto Douglas* & Eric Garner**

When the elephant
Throws its weight on the ant
In the tingling harmony of green forests
Can it breathe?

When the cow Tramples on the cat
Owner of all in a rat's stomach
Can it breathe?

When the snuffed horse
Throws off its rider
Seals the steaming charge
With desperate hoofs

Is the centre of the earth
Not broken in bits and pieces?

Garish prickling seizes the wind
Dumb kindling slakes the spirit
Warped in the roots, rusty foliage
 In the clatter of raindrops.

The snooty closets, fetish gravitas
The aborigine judders in the chokehold
On the margins of oil mangroves
In the drowsy moonlight.

---

* Foremost Niger Delta activist
** The desperate plea "I can't breathe" is attributed to Eric Garner who was
  choked to death by a New York City policeman in 2014

O the drowning straws, inverted glories
The frothy deals, ripening percentages
Such shrikes on land
Shriving in lambent sweetness!

The ruddy revelation:
The earth lapses from lack of love;
The cribbed voice
Is incapable of green codes.

O heavenly beings, come down
Probe the harpy blood
The orgiastic instincts
The faithful fallow and famished.

THE FIESTA OF BLOOD

No one agrees, in the beginning,
Some migrations,
Even in their distilled form,
Take us to a dead end,
Sometimes, a headless trip to the sky.

The wind, intangible aid of flight Is,
itself, a consummate vortex
Full of guile and grit-
An open thicket hiding scorpions.

The mind is the motor of all motions
Responds post-haste to triggers of blood
The nincompoop bloated by stuff
Beats his chest before doting in-laws

Riding luxurious paratroops in the air
And how he loves hairy hounds
Trapping them down
In their zipped hideouts
Not caring a hoot about the quilt...

The ebbing tempo of the phallus
At old age obsessed
With seasonless things
But a snake must prove its worth
 Or turns rope for tying firewood...

Cramp spoils the fiesta of blood
And the sump of being waxed
In skyscrapers without ventilation
Or song or annotations.

Across the ages,
Blood soars on burnt wings
God never raised sons from sand
To carry the cross
On the way to Golgotha.

RUBBLE IN THE TIDE

The sappy forbearance
 The earth speaks of
In her husky voice
That distils chaff and rum.

The matriarch avoids altercations
 In the village square;
The tongue mothers an open fart
Though there is fire in apathy, foetus

Of an unaltering downward slide
Like a fallen angel in the outposts
Primed with smoke, punctual poke
Of onion in the eyes

Showing a haggard iron will,
 A model's perfect foil
On the stage of blood
Larger than the birds' sky.

O the unflagging fabrications in the air
The disorienting claims of invincibility
Benighted and blunt and boisterous
In their niggling dreamland.

The sweet solicitude thrust on self
Stalking neighbours in the spirit world
Recondite and turbulent and monstrous
This thralldom ends in empty treasuries.

The seats in the assemblies empty of sap
An eerie mantra enriches the honeycomb
 A radial of ponderous shadows
Holding the lamp and mirror.

The inheritance is halved in broad daylight
 The clustering of white-apparelled crooks
Cackling, like black and white pigeons
In their radiance and wholesome teak

The silent ones and their swollen scrotums
Shine on the sidelines
Basking in the backwoods
Soaked in grieving ends

The rubble floats in the tide
Winsome in their wobble
In the bedlams of the earth
Where flowers grow without toil...

I remember the plundered ponds of my roots
The incandescent darkness wrought on homes
 Where palm wine taints the senses
Wet *garri* and milk kill its powers.

THE MAP OF HONEYCOMBS

See the luminous maze between her legs
Bearer of cataclysm in the blood
Melter of towering rocks in the sun –
The bee can draw the map of honeycombs.

A dissembled memory whirls in the soul
Man becomes sodden and turgid
At the same time
Drowning the magnificence of the rose

In muddy gutters
Or the dove's dizzying gait
 In dry, black thickets
The anonymity of voices heard in the sky

The tumid warmth floating in the harmattan
The patrimony of strange mates
A wincing echelon in flow tide
A wilful sputtering of the Arts.

O floundering scribblers of bonfires
Spoilers of God's word in the arena
Their bland propositions riddled
With thunderstorms and wasps and brambles!

What is poetry with no culture content
Or salt or living burnish?
A litany of flashy odium
A rusty participle in the dark

A benighted pubescence
Arts, when indigestible, becomes a lump;
Simply hangs in the throat
The muse is scythed in moonlight.

The sellouts and moonchasers and microchips
Devour its every bit, cancelling out
The native alphabet, the mental harpoon
Torpedoes its benign propensities

Leave your house unswept at dawn
A hanging debt you must pay on return;
Is a bird perching on an anthill
Not on the ground?

Is a fellow with one wife
Not with one mind?
Do we break the waterpot
 Because it is rainy season?

So strange blood grows
 In a man at old age?
The metallic parts and the gothic
Cram the air; pick the crumbs

In grilled outdoor menus and witness
The gratuitous slip into briefcases
Of the west they carry with gusto
Forever undiscovered from clime to clime

Open their synthetic phallus
In unfailing serials, strangle
The bitches revelling on Bomadi beach
The bulging Iscariots, the posh locomotives

And habitations on the highway
Partying with the ancestors astride River Thames in twilight,
lapping up
The virginal coziness through the backdoor

    Who can save the sappy song
    Lighting up the fireplace
    In the dark, dank night?

The galloping grasshopper
Cannot be a threat
To the praying mantis.

A SORCERER'S RAINBOW

They soar on trenches
These preeners of the earth
Watching barns blistering in the wind;
 A sorcerer's rainbow
Cruises on earth, not above

Forgetting a gravedigger always drifts
 With no undulating rockscape
Or corpses of dissolute origins,
Beyond catechists' glasses,
Whinnying here and there.

The pricking aperture in the soul
The unhealing sore in the blood
Boomerang with no trace;
The *agbọrọ gbẹin owu*[*]
Chases away hunger from the land-

Unflagging blossoms Like cocoyam leaves
In a garbage dump
But who swallows sugarcane
Goaded on by its sweetness?

The spirit is dressed in multi-coloured pyjamas
Walks on the tides of life
In asymmetrical bridles
Obtrusive voices in the background
The deference of a self-effacing professional.

---

[*] A kind of masquerade

They act on impulse
Rupturing the song –
 Or are dead to it;
The stagnating flotsam of inner diffidence
A sweet- sounding nutriment without intonation

Leading conceits well up in disguise
 Unaltering, like God's sign on skin
Unfalsifiable, like the scriptures
Though Chimeras in all their gloss
Turn rubble in the mirror.

This poem is a prophetical primer
 Smashed in the spine
A damp dream in a sunny night
In a slovenly latchet, a humble
Nondescript swagger in the soul

Robed in naked vessels of light
 Like an old woman
Dispelling the bloats in the joints
 Like flooded shorelines
In the Niger Delta, in moonshine.

The ditty disposition of a lunatic
On the highway, humming homewards
(which hardly exists)
The radiant rhetoric, ponderous rhymes
Of cadavers and conmen and insidious boardrooms

In the middle of night
Of memorable edifices; full of seduction
There is no inheritance without a shadow
Benevolent bedlams
Soaring and soaring into clouds.

HOW DOES ONE KILL A BUTTERFLY IN FLIGHT?

As kids in the seventies
We crabbed and oystered and kotoed
 On the bounteous Bomadi beach
Cracking eggs for a prize on somnolent wings

Beyond conjugal bliss in a wet night
Oblivious of the seedy byways and sandstorms
Choking chains and chaff
Mocking God's handmaidens in sunlight.

Moods were straight with sap
Clapping for the tailor
Who, compulsive of conscience, kept the promise –

How does one kill a butterfly in flight
And not court the wrath of the gods?

Nowadays, a credulous discretion
Labours to find nutriment
For the bond of brothers
Needing a nudge in the navel

To halt the hallowed flesh from flight –
Fertile ground for the grey moments
Swallowing the stranded world
In deep measured gulps

To halt the sewage of airs
And the tepid tongue

Flowering aches
Limpid groans
Thawing dreams
Nifty knuckles

And the shibboleths
Painting phantom dreams
In the sky
in the crisp turbulence of high tide.

Who does not know
The birdsong is a barricade
Ruining the stairs to a hilltop

The delightsome flute
In the air
Only cloaks the wreck in paradise?

Sometimes, the mask is open
In the marketplace
Even in retreat, its naked shadow
Sets the barns ablaze, inhabiting

Blameless newborns,
In the hypnotic forbearance
Of an alcohol- propelled sanity
Sputtering the song on the highway

Sometimes, it whirls in its shrouds
In the avowed compassion of a maniac
Countersigning the noological lyrics
Of a matron, dandling a scurrilous place

Distinct in a cold kind of way
Catechists and absent miracles in the cathedral
They are always clad in lubberly sanctimony
Always voluptuous in the stomach

Their towering heights bear no fruits
The strides remain an illusion;
The solicitude can win the heart
Of a hardened pharaoh

Like the hunter,
They *scatter* their traps in the forest
 As the antelope
Scatters its legs.

The welter of bones and melting props
 Fate of the choleric in all spaces;
In this monastery in the wind
Conclusions come without a conference

The frontiers and foremen tango
The Knots and nothingness unfaltering
A secret love blossoms
Soiled in sin, diminishing the spirit

And the crowded street
Is trapped in mortal arms
The schemers brandish catholic chaplets
Dislimning the sacrilege in the air

When an oracle demands for fowl
After a heavy meal of goat for years
Can the worshippers still bank on
The ancestors' unbroken breath?

The air pines for healing
In the arms of the rain;
The soft shower raking aside
The black debris rippling the blood

Of otherwise seasoned sages
Leaving them limping
In the whirlwind
Nibbling their singed souls.

MAN AND MERMAID

The flickering sainthood in patches of sunrise
The symmetrical steps before the camera
Like *Olorogun* in a leg-twisting dance
After the sprinkling of water
Three times on the headpiece.

The disturbing spectacle
 Of a white bungalow
Showing off colourful flowers
Without a roof;

The mermaids do have
A hand in this matter:
Is a sick soul, as they say,
Not the prophet's slave?

Ensconced in this water paradise
Without doorways, their bond
With man is somewhat obtuse
Scribbled down in eternal long hand
The differentials startle even the foot soldiers.

The speck in it all continues
To etch in memory, edging towards
The shadow of things
Spawned in the bristling dark

Cosy velleities without known preludes
Or follow-ups
Like an impassioned fling
 In a hot, hot afternoon

In a sailing ship
To resurrect the senses
Like a good theatre of cracked visions
Carried in mellow tones
On the seashore

In open cornets, to rub
It into the medulla oblongata-
 Receptacle of sprinting joys
Like the full- tide excitement

Of spectators when *Olorogun*,
Inching towards the river
For the water sprinkling ritual,
Suddenly stops in his tracks,

Like a horse seeing what is in front
Beyond ordinary eyes...

A BLOOD DESIRE

A blood desire has no ears,
Like the phallus,
 Its muzzle rests on the wind
Where it spits white counterpoints
 Into an unfillable bin

And a snaky smoke sails
 Through the window
To the azure sky
Licking up infantile daylight

Like an unwilling damsel
Like an undecided toast
The hand perennially held up
By the mounting moods in the world.

Who would want
 To ruffle feathers
And end the journey
In the middle of the moon
Or in cathartic sidelines

Formulated in high seas
 In full tide
To tease out love
From the rubble

Or wriggling on the back,
Like an upturned cockroach
 In a tiny corner
At the village cathedral

Visible only with lamplight;
A scudding sprawl
An absent- minded ardour
Or a mutinous memory
Of refined claws' caresses?

BROKEN TIDE I

Stellar outings, deflating harvests
A flustering song in oozing armpits
Abrasive icons, murderers of loaded rivulets
No fire blazes in the hearth forever,

Withering into a cold wreck –
A heap of feathers moss in the tide,
Waltzing into a timeless accent

Sentiments as rough as a tiger's tongue
Sink without seam in silent seas
Over a keg of overnight frothy palm wine.

Always, the dream beyond the roof
Is hemmed in by the slick
Of a collapsed staircase
The hedge broken in the middle of the song

The swill of bush birds
Flapping their wings in towering spheres
 In mid- air, in jocund joy

As picturesque as baby *Olorogun*
Rhythmically striking
Leg rattles before his father.

You can say, like cancer
Maniacal minds blacken the bubble
Beyond the gods' splatter
In dark waters beyond

The slovenly snags, terrestrial
 Squeaking in the owl's shriek
In the dead of night

Delighting the gods of glitches
Like unwashed utensil
Swimming fish on Bomadi shores at dawn.

The deserted compunctions
Lying fallow in human blood
The woeful vestures
Sourcing humus

From fishbone, the sightless gales
And thunderbolts and cramps
In the depths of the river.

To prosper in their pockets
Don't they pine for pogroms
From underseas and overseas

Do they know the damsel
That spurns advances
Saves us from debt?

Here to the inner propellers of the soul
Which shape the dance in the wind
No computer can measure penance

The bubbling miasma of exhalation
 Of caked black stuff from the bowels,
Ascending to freedom on mountaintops

Here to the fellowship of alleluia beings-
The green goblet of God's ultimate gift
Ungathered by failing blood, begetting
A tale of splintering memories.

BROKEN TIDE II

The proletariat seeks full lives in cathedrals
Foliage in full bloom, dissymmetry
Of interposing storms and outcrops
Scalding the serenity of the soul
In secular spheres.

Who does not need a salutary mood,
Sequined in upward migrations?
Votive petals always seize the mind
Even in destitute clothes!

No sane blood finds harmony with harpoons
O let our feet find dew
Even in heated crossroads
Abstract riddles do not have a loose end
Nothing to cobble into the cob.

Doesn't the toddler wonder
At the wincing pain
The adult exudes over his bite?
Put your hand into the tortoise's anus
 And see the reward!

Threshed in opacity
Life remains a prayer field
A surfeit of squandering and slime
Contrasting the craft of cricket sounds
At Bomadi beach, in the hues of dawn.

The bubbles on River Forcados
Sometimes presages self-entanglement
Habitual loathing of the middle course
Who gains what
From perpetually standing on edge?

The river's broken tide is a bludgeoning
Haunch exhaled by the wind
Disheveller of still chattels
Rechristened by flags and rhetoric

The inner waywardness, the drowning gusto
Livid pestilence they hew
On a pageant of butterflies
Nothing prefigures the presence of earthquakes
Only the dismemberment of outgrowths.

Piety deserts the pulpit and her moorings
 Like sunken suitors sauntering away
From a mountainous dowry
A finical desire to undo self
Burning in the spirit, primed hovels of flesh

Their prayers are pommels of wounded earth,
Spores of motley grace
The heartland swollen and peppery
Like skin stung by bees
The choirmasters coarse in their flinty notes

Parochial in their niceties
The hurray of impotent aphrodisiac
Halo of hell debouching excitedly
In the colours of a monarch butterfly
Breeding cadavers, compost of worm-infested summits

Adamant meshes of power and hate
The soft entreaties before the vote
Signalling our matter
Is on a tree top

The ossified attitude on the seat
Even the snake can take a new skin
In the sun- starveling inanities of the spirit
Fireless hearths, ebbing footholds.

BATTLEFIELD

The world slides eons underground,
Unknowingly,
In the encumbering battles
Of the soul in full tide –

A benign cherub carrying
A pile of charcoal plots
Covert and blazing
Built with brain and blood.

The clatter of suppressed fardels
Scrupulous like a loud cloud
The ticklish sun of vanities
Seasoned fabrications in the pulpit

Licking up sumptuous petals
Like the famished shorelines of the delta
This world is a shadow emblazoned
Groaning in the sun

The muddied air of a toddler
On a mountaintop in a dream
The demagogue's vainglory props up
The history of unborn ages, thumping their niches

Cold hearths flare up
Without prompting, or a jab
In an unending festival of tripe
Inhaling the black light in the air

A landscape of a lunatic aroma
A scalding green without form
A glossy charcoal, a picturesque jungle
Steeped in brine and grime

A brimless market of ghosts
A blossoming graveyard at twilight
A tumid wreck, estranged dandy
Bubbling in his strides in the abetting sun

Deflecting the curses
Of a naked woman
On the riverbank
Who has always been used

And dumped by her supposed lovers
A vesture of black colours and indiscretion
An empty oesophagus, a gradation
Of flailing infinitude, faltering lanterns

In the scallop of earthy schemes
Filaments of tickling bargains
Crashing, cracking, hallowing
Slides in fulsome fragrance.

Earthly patriots sundered in the blood
Truncated in their tracks
In the swelling underseas of their being
By urchins who are high flyers.

HUSKS OF MEMORY

An obtrusive memory of the soul
 At the peak of his flairs and guts
Slain in the middle of the rains
In the blazing darkness

Swallowing the crescent moon
The accompanying pulsations urge the maker
To remake or rechristen the world
Or simply rupture their stride.

An army of green
Swarms the rustling reeds
Full of fire and fury
Aiming fastidious bullets
At the blood of urchins

Otherwise abstract beings
Magnified in the marketplace,
Forever answerable to
The somnolence of light

The gust of terrestrial whims
The blind votes and conflagrations

Spouting up geraniums and small fires
Buried deep in canals and riverbeds
The canoe splintering and floundering
In the swill of obdurate birds at night

Turbid notaries, parishioners of shadowy psalms
A merchandise of cellars in the spirit
 Extracted from bones and braids and brooms
 The guitarist comes nursing a sore

       Sauce to rhythms of the soul
       Sauce to emblazoned perfumes
       And the maniac's fastidious blackness
        In the prompt flotilla of memory

The husks of inconsolable gambits
And their shadows, the harrowing havens
The legion of flowery ponds, floating
On a cannonade splintered in the teeth.

The owl clambers a whispering palm tree
The sun at its peak, the geometry of ruin
Gnawing at silky skins, the blistered palms
Without therapeutic aprons or poppies.

Devour the quintessence of flighty pigeons
Disservers of the lair in the sun
Uncouple laughter in secret corners
Stoking eternal fires in pleasant places

Tasteless, lengthening the hazards
 Pitfalls of greying foams in the sea
Announce the pith of mariners
In the nakedness of a broken tripod.

A FRUITAGE OF SHADOWS

The empty caverns in times of Corona
Mess up the dominion of howitzers
And manless drones in the sky, like shoes
Without stockings, or a fitting leg.

Laughter does not grow in a graveyard
The undying stones and cactus
Swell towards the silent sea
Dissolve the millennial cupola

The world wears like a pendant
 The arcane fruitage of shadows

The sedulous pomegranate, prying
At the onlooker and the fannies
The nakedness of a starry damsel
In infinite mindless nights of loitering

The genial dissonance, the irregular notes
Of the amethyst on mountain tops
Eyelashes and thighs that drag one
Towards the obsidian deep

A labyrinthine place;
Full and empty at once:
Do not put your head inside –
Since Adam broke the yolk

No one has filled the hole
In the middle of the earth
Sumptuous without salt
A crystal matrix, a vagrant mantle

A perfumed prison, scalding aroma
A gratuitous waist crammed with slippage
In the meadows, in the moment of reckoning
Dismembers blood brothers

A brimless ferment
And heckle on the corridor
Threshers have no patience in moonlight –
 Famishing hermetics and honey

How they squander
A patrimony of armorial victories!
The stripped primordial effulgence
The ravishing strains in the vineyard

The scales in the eyes and seedy summits
 In the break of day
The skirmishes that ruin the windshield

Steeped in darkly hooves;
 Lodestones, visible and fragrant
Sundered tides and thrushes and alleyways
The sullen harbours and soothing aprons

The slothful vocation of digging pits
To bury the moonlight laced with incense
Among implacable cherubs and stockade
Among flowering gentiles.

BUBBLING MARKETS

Laurels these days
Are hinged on fake hedges
Harried niceties, debouching
In the wilderness, gaunt coconut heads
Turned idols of the sweltering incense.

An extravagant surplice, looking succulent
On the surface; hazy dons bequeath
A blind bastion; a tangled python
Ruler of the jungle – owner of the torrents
Of hailstone in the night.

The ditches spout up the rubble
The grief overwhelms the backwaters
The vanquished fear no funeral
No cannonade; no vampire

No holocaust or crimson jabs
No battering by bullets or brigands
A fastidious whorl of undercurrents
Enjoy the amplitude of the sun
In the company of crocs and Cains

The ultimate despair is in town,
The uttermost sparkle
Of funeral drums in a wet night
Throbbing in the hearth of plantain shrubs
Squalls of honeymoons and pathways

The drowning columns in the village cathedral
Accustomed to dry unfurling in the wilderness
Salutary venoms in flower buds
An anonymous bloodthirsty brood
Blooms into moonlight

II
Angels dwell on earth
Stained with salt and dew
Seedlings of light and silver
Uncouple the heathen with a kiss
On the temple...

Patriots are a ferment restrained
Cut short; spoilers of bubbling markets
Haunches cluster around the carrion
Confirmed in conferences of cronies
Strangulators of long necks

The stripping league of big walking sticks
In a landscape dampened
With armpit sweat and scent
The wilting herbage in the bay
The futile agitations and the deaf

The sea gods swaying on land
The sour pieties and barricades.

COCKING THE STRUGGLE

The wrinkled whore is a deserted breed
Importunate leafage and flower pots
Go sore in broken tide
Steering away the sunbird

The tawny circle of heavy weights
Are always scared of the turn of fortune

Swelling the unbreakable scallop of stalls
The sedulous bargains in the rock
The detonations of benign propositions
The belfries, the sacred candles at night

Decreeing longevity in power
Burnishing coarse moustaches
Back their bulbous directions with half- truths
Staving off high voltage skirmishes.

The congregation of sullen urchins
Living on promises, their gripping green
Pulsing in the seas, darkening the sparkle
 Road marshals, too, crash their helmets.

II
The armed lad is stripped
Weighs nothing on the scale
After the gory showing of guts and grits
Cocking the struggle,

Unfazed in the clouds
                            In the cold,
                            In the river,

In the night

The commanders suck the honey
Right in the beehives
And beyond and beside
The lad, anonymous and wanton
 Battles the memory of stones
Like owners of burnt Onitsha market stalls.

One must raise motes in the mind
Dealing with hearts of stone;
Rifles and gunpowder find solace
In grim pastimes, in sullen darkness

Hanging on a cliff, the harrowing cross
The broken lustre of the soul
The stampede of reason, the satiny stuff
After the storm, after the strain

Always, there is a ferment restrained
In tumid essences and tunnels
Beyond the darkening tattoo
The broken niches, torrents
Of nameless notaries with big briefcases

The allegorical primer holds sway,
The death of a winging swallow
The pusillanimous ritual queues
Impotent in the peeking sun
The dour incandescence of bones.

SUNBURNT HEIGHTS

Who will dare disfigure the fun;
The knowing stare of moonlight
 In funeral nights: postulants
Playing with the opposite sex
In plantain shrubs on Mount Everest?

Man is entangled in sunburnt heights
A possessed counterpoise
Unyielding to the turn of the tide;
The aroma of slain blood lives long
In the nostrils of a conquistador

And the craving for darkly things
Even in light bludgeons
The tambourines and nightgowns:
When the paternoster is said in the cathedral
Harried spirits flood the stonehouse

The voice is cradled to give verve
To perduring tastes
And the cutting off of peering necks
The shadowy pianos, the winking eyelashes
The lachrymose inanities of destitute beings

The obdurate blood in dry caverns
Afloat on rosebuds and allegiances
The arena of flowerless blooms
Pontifical latitudes and toasts

The trappings of fraternities
O a tree lives in the centre of town
Where night men bury

Their sins and crevices and pustules
When the whitewashed mask sleeps
With angels of light in the arms of the rain
All is fathom, figurehead altitudes
Transcendental incest, like
Graft garnished like Christmas garments

And flowers track the vulnerable
In the cathedral garden
Whittling down the genial syllable of being
The silent music of flow-tide.

Alibis and funfairs do not show heroism
The ponderous think beyond funeral wreaths
Or the rainbow of catches
That court home hounds

Primed on chaliced choices in the rain
The devil's xylophone thrives in detours
Fathoms of flight, saltless skies
The endless moans in high-flying markets.

There is no staircase to light
Only moral guitarists
Know the painted steps
Surrounded by crickets and cicadas
Beyond the brine and grime in the wind

Gobbling up the sizzling memory
Of *Itoko*⁺ pepper-soup and oil-garri
At Binebai's place in Burutu-
The flawless Island*

⁺ A type of fish
* Burutu is otherwise known as the island of no regrets. Whether the

Whose rotund feast
Now hangs on oblique shadows
Sprouted from black blood and chaff
In nocturnal boardrooms.

present state of the island justifies the sobriquet or not, is another matter
altogether.

GREEN IS ALWAYS IN WILD FORESTS

I
A Jehovah's witness could fall
For a smoking dude;
Every season is harvest time
In the delirious mind,
Firing fates to twin-tower heights.

No estrangement
To those who have mastered
The labyrinthine creeks
Of the human mind

Incandescent edifices
Lying fallow in living boardrooms
The doleful thrombosis
Spell the beauty of blood

The labyrinth and moral supplements
The lichen in parallel undergrounds
The flinching obsidian symmetry
Slumbering like a newborn in nature's arms.

Providence retrieves the carnations in sunburns
Precipitate pathways, sodden nakedness;
The milky silence rowing
In an expansive sea

    In a dream
     Without paddles
    Against the tide
    In the dead of night.

II

A sick man bare to the bones
By *angala*[*] fireside and his herbs
Regains the glow of the goldfish
 Limning the light of his voice,
Blithesome, like a sunbird drunk with nectar.

There is always
An expendable hype
In the crunch moment

Like wrestlers' *Ogele*[+]
The blaze over armament
Against Covid- 19, strapped

To a nebulous expenditure and fabrications
The actors in cloud nine;
Green is always in wild forests

Covering whirlpools and stumps
Thorns and thistles and black waters
 Flowing in complicit canals.

_____

[*] Mangrove wood
[+] Procession

VACUOUS LIGHT

Bubbles dance on fate,
On visions of rain fading away
In filthy vintage steads and nettles, withering

On the temple wherein lies
Harried Footprints; taciturn,
Open-minded bursts of petals.

The world is a shadesome tree
With perfumes of ancient obscenities
Lingering bonfires without pianos or ribbons
Swagger of unleavened souls
In ever- blossoming meadows

The carnival of flowery migrations
In underground plateaus and deserts
The showmanship in minefields
Stifling water and fish in the soul
Full of speck and freckle.

II
Always, heartbeats suffer
A maul in their blaze
In their flowering and blossom
In their abiding sizzle –
Loneliness hounds like a leopard

Nothing bitter or furtive
Or ambiguous about it, after all;
Just the debarked emptiness

And squandering and squawking
Or gawking of actors and interferers
Or gossips the police
Have no warrant to stem, like
The fossilization of a tsetse fly on the skin
The motionlessness packed in despondency

And a flint in the blood
A blossoming furrow, stained with light
With the intensity of a snail's movement
Marks the takeover of grazing fields

Hardly a grain is left on the gaze
The mash of tiny pores
Underline the vacuous lights in the marketplace
But even stones flower in the mind

And forgotten robes adorn a dandy
On the day of the king's coronation;
Witches gather in broad daylight
To decide the fate
Of the blossoming casseroles.

O the triumphal vehemence of predation
Like cocks on cockroaches; fountains
Exuding artificial wrinkles,
Unseen squadrons
Decimate the greenery in the air!

The sages may be just right
As they always seem to be:
What befalls another
Befalls a piece of wood!

HONEY WITHOUT BEES

I

Uncouple the stones, or break them;
Life must have a bearing
Even in the ebb tide of a virus –
Honey can grow out
Of fingernails and cadavers.

The patrimony of salt and water
Without blood-letting or larvae
Defining their contours
But the constellations run rings around
Closed doors and esoteric syllables.

This world has no steering;
No dew- drenched pollens

The plinth in the song of the heathen
The virginal ruminations

Burning on the shoreline
Ditch plans for a furlough on headlands.

II

Bolt the door against posers
Sitting on the royal throne
When the blue blood squirms on the floor.

This is a tentative trench in the cold
Though acidulous and sweet- smelling
Solid facades flash fleeting fragrance

On the face of the earth.
Empty petticoats remain awake
To the planet's burden and menace
Aiming without caution
Even with a single bullet

The swarming trifles, insensate self-hood
The celebration of a big catch
In the skein of drought and squalor

The surfeit of seizures and greenless fields
A lapse always gnaws at wholesome recesses
Strips the gunman of his precision
The poetics of piety and pestilence.

The smutty radiance in the sun,
Like Bomadi sandbanks
Phosphorescent and extravagant and primed
And inviting, needing no foreplay
Before the plunge; unfading

Petals of destitute hues
Devouring the *kpokpo* garri*
And roasted fish

The family had prepared for Easter –
The fastidious table manners
The quintessence of twisted primers

The satanic dealings in havens
The padlocked bawling in charted corners
Snuffing out the essence of being

---

* Cassava flakes – a staple food in the Niger Delta.

On planet earth, like Corona...

The threat as fleshy as spilled fuel
Causes generator fire
But blood can multiply cicadas
And butterflies on broken wings.

A SWARM OF BEINGS

Here is a white will
To migrate
From soot- draped modes
To ultimate greenery in the wild –
Flowers grow on a leopard's claw.

Slothful lights take a million centuries
To clear the debris which reinvents itself
Like the swelling, oozing sludge
In my neighbourhood gutter, underlining

The gross blundering,
The trumpery across the seas
Holding fast to the ladder of descent.

The legion of trivial births In the manger in moonlight
Smouldered even before breath begins
The cross currents visible in the dark
The closed doorways and smoke

The perfidy and the pantheress
The abiding thunderstorms
And shattered glasses
Newborns suck breasts without nipples
Bubbling in the ambiguous waters

Lodestones and slaughter slabs
When the conquistador nestles in causeways
The detonations in the air a routine
Burnishing shadows of selfhood.

II

Here is a swarm of beings
On the high sea to heaven
The spoiler, stinging stuff to stupor
A dishevelling contrivance blazing

Like a sharpened machete in the sun
The lightning unnerving the symmetry
Of the restoration strides in glory land
Prefigures the ascent of a lion

Speed boats glide on the River Nun
And sharks of all shapes and colours
The merger of fishes and hippos
In the undercurrents

The weltering phosphorescence
Needs rechristening
Freedom breathes under a trample
In one brackish settlement

Pusillanimous motions crowd the assemblies
The quarrels and fence-jumping gimcrack
 The hollow immensity of icons
Living in a closet of sorts-

All pillars of stomach business.
O who can define the dying footfalls
Of the vague, anonymous constituent
O n a weft of the earth.

BLESSED BLOOD IN THE CREEKS

In Letugbene creek
Near fatuous beings bathe
In spillage and squalor
Spawned by flow stations
And casseroles
Bullets and brigands.

The odium of a blessed blood
Swallowed by bales of debauchery –
Compatriots sweat in the rain
To free themselves, like *Olorogun*[*]
Struggling for disentanglement
From the grip of cult members.

No one hears a hollow growl
In the labour room;
Satan hates bonfires and staircases
 Kindled by a haul of flighty doves

The boundless green banners
The cartographic musings, the buffoonery
Masked as a masterpiece of craft,
Unfold their darkly wings in the waters

Brusque fates; the devil incarnate
Drowns souls in the incandescent sea
After removing the big intestine

---

* The biggest masquerade in Ayakoromo.

The gout of earthquakes around little tendrils
The defenceless remains the accused
A prisoner of slovenly intellection
Plundered harvests, shifting signposts
Like waves undulating in the middle.

EARTHLY SAINTS

Medals and plaques
Adorn sitting rooms of earthly saints
A carnival of multiplication in the wind
A menacing mirage
Full of bugle, emblematic of nothing.

A mere floss or contrived meadows
Uncoupled from a bouquet of feathers
And delirious pathways
Overlords of the underbrush

The geology of creased fates
And the falling sickness in the market place –
 Just get acquainted with stones
And the sting of wasps
On the scrotum.

The moon loves the company
Of backbiters and sycophants and plain knaves
Emblazoning the comic canvas (in the harmattan wind)
Spurning the calcareous calculations

Nurtured by greed, the gauntlet of dominion
And its abiding grey aura in lean spheres;
The mutilations of god's green
Stem from a whorish kind of ineptitude
Or the very lack of circumspection in the wild.

GODLY GREED

A clot of capering dreams
On a white canvas
Remains a baggage hoisted in the sun
Slovenly dispositions mull over the tide
Denounce cannons and crowns.

A banquet of failed experiments
Litter aerated archives in fatherland
The withering amphibious food amplifies itself
 In the unfailing cusp of oiled rhetoric.

The flower of blood
Turns a conical creed
In the arms of the rain
Sometimes a howling cloud.

Teach my unborn child
The arithmetic of a godless greed

The patriarchs ditch the cadences
Of the godhead and the gusts of green
They grew up with in dreamy meadows
Hedged by vagrant vegetation

And the sweet- smelling freezing
Of the early morning breeze
At the waterside, pumping life into skeletons.
Now, this air is fouled by the burst

Of want on farts and contrived grey

Deep gorges ripple its purity
The rock flares up to the sky
 In the gale of hate speech
A subtle reminder the husk
 Is king of the wind

Sycophants, pestiferous in their calligraphy
Bow to the synthetic babble of bureaucrats
 Who dress the table for the overlords-
A flash of swarthy incest in high places

The knot of unearned allowances
Kneads festivals of gutter and lustre
The cast iron silvery gaits
On the corridors of their slippage

The grilled ostrich alibis and crosses
The litany of red rainfalls
The watery magnitude of molluscs
The putrefaction of motionless drainages

The parallel chimneys without smoke
Filing out; the spine of submarines and lulls
The vile estrangement howling underground
The sodden labyrinths between thighs

So transparent in the dark
Celestial strides; a frail importunity
Floating in a crocodile- infested pond
The dismemberment of full- blooded cathedrals

Squatting somewhere in the mind
The sarcophagus lies supine
The walls littered with flailing webs

And rat's brine and skeleton.
Nothing compares to the bravado
Of the smug in spirit wearing a mask
To teach the world how to swim on land-
Is a sick man not the prophet's slave?

THIS CORROSIVE SYLLABLE

The figurehead claims ownership of the stage
Covering unimaginable mileages in slow strides
Such steady trappings and damnation
Which outsider ponders the secrets of *Owobou!**

The effacing landlord makes do
With the foyer unseen at the back
Avoiding the menace of louting masquerades
Burnished by fate's fiendish hand

The corrosive syllable of hand-made freckles
Shuts the door against light
In seething sobriety; everything
Is timed in the patrimony of shadows

Even the waves cease to roll
En route the shoreline weeds
When the satiny wind sails away
The frontiers adorned with faeces

The delectation and smile drown
In invisible black waters
Occasionally plodding death
In choleric morning dews.

---

* Masquerade forest

II

Drive away the weft of blood and salt
The sobbing child rejects sagged breasts
The sheer lack of scintillation and seasoning
Not the green charm of hanging water melons

The ponderous patriot is in labour
To swallow the stony sauce in public
The monstrous discretion of a serpent
 And tangible bad breath

The saints are always in cassock
 Like smog on the cathedral roof
Servicing the stagnation floating in the air
The lifeless leafage on the seashore

The weight of fleshy illusion
Dandles a devious nutriment of the soul –
Desultory and powerful –
The conqueror's essence towers in their calculus

Carbonized angels take flight
In a fleecy fondling of lubberly bald heads
Faltering, like a benighted ballad
Scarred in quicklime contours.

HUSKS OF BECOMING

I
An invented vainglory,
The abiding smell of Rambo
Riddled with slippage; it is no longer news
The sky hides scythes in her bosom.
The gonad of godly goofs in the air;

This treasure is handled like eggs
The familial girdle and supplements
The terrestrial lichens and faltering
On waterways, in an insensate gout

Unmaking the cavernous beatitude
Of the riverside and woodlands
And the light of day recoils like a mamba
Without hitting the target
The expired venom, the laborious lemons

Of chastity finding no home in the world
Though honeycombs litter her navel
No trickle of moonlight openness and pathways
A devious impulse abounds, in reeking shrouds

The saddlery apparel glitters through the dark
Prostitution takes over the pulpit
The patrimony of pilfering
The foul latitude, the raddle of bald fabrications

The forbearance, the dreamy meadow
Itself a tricky beast, the heritage
Of the cherub, drenched
In glitches in a licentious freewill.

II
Summon the decorum of ancients
Unwritten, engraved in translucent tides
The wayward mothering
Throws pebbles at the peeking sun

Estranges the living light of the beginning
 Eternal spine of anonymity and incense
Underground honeycombs shudder
At the dynamite exploding in the soul

The votary maze slams the door
Against festivities, in silence,
To harden the godhead like pharaoh
The succulent streets witness black rain

Drowning the countless caverns of the earth.
Listen to the babbling and trifle
The pulverized moonlight
The shattered order of ripe breasts.

THE FIREFLY TICKLES THE NIGHT

In the secret melody of the bedroom
One hears crackling laughter
But the meadows are disconsolate
The ruminants have their limit.

The firefly tickles the night
 But her tranquil trappings
Are stripped to bare bones
By man's pitch- black tenderness

Peddling thorns in place of tendrils
Decomposed corpses in place of dewdrops
 Littering rickshaws and flow stations –
Delusion has a prize in black rain

The imperial opium and distractions
In full moon, in green waters
The shadow emblazons the dance –
 The inner propeller of the soul

Tickling abettors, resolute and pontifical
A maudlin sacrifice to Satan
A counterfeit sauce, in the tusk of the mind
Lachrymose and devious and despoiled.

There is no chlorophyll in the greenery
Stills the flight of butterflies
Credulous in midair; it is a needless conceit
 Poured on a fast- flowing tide

Precipitates phoney elevation
The stairs of the wind complicit
A cluster of blood-thirsty goddesses
Spew a heft of benighted tidings.

In prickly play in moonlight
Torrents of blood trussed to the heart

Whoever propagates the complementation
Of the sexes in the wind
Shuts out acid rain and hailstone
With a torn umbrella

The muddy essences down the silvery sea
Pure knaves have their way
In darkly blaze, dismantling
The garrisons of earthly incandescence.

TICKLES AND THUNDERBOLTS

I
The gravedigger's secret prayer is well known
Plunges conquistadors into foul waters
The crepuscular formations dedicated to the sea god
The fecundity of grey on the landscape.

Let us uncouple the adamant ribs
The raw saturnine heart of the believer
 The foliage in the wind
Withers in the armpit

Harbouring tickles and thunderbolts
The coarseness of stone in the sun
And the age- long longing for the moon
On the niggling notes of a piano.

The faint- hearted surrenders to painted brambles
Draining blood and dream
Haters of imperial affinities promote
 Incandescence in rusted herbage.

There is no sky without shadows
Lovers do not see the slimy stones
On the seashore
The wild thickets in sweet- smelling forests
The crocodile in the depths of River Forcados.

II
Earth's palette is a mixed grill in the sun
The snake abandons its disused skin
The pot minds not its soot
Grim rubble floats in unscrupulous torrents

Dark smoke snakes lustily
 To the high heavens;
No fathoms, no extravagant rings or cloaks
On bare sore, spouting up surplices.

Patriots grow big on graft
Earthquakes and volcanoes and viruses
And riverbeds take more blood
Than mortal battles.

A fardel unravels nothing after the search
Sweltering stars oversee barren brooks
And thorny black foliage; a hollow headmaster
 Cloaks the official gulf with niceties

A scrupulous catechist fondles aphrodisiac
And the rosary in dire supplication in the dark
The scarlet footfalls in graveyards
The hallowed middens with no mind for remedy.

BLACK PIANOS

The pestilence in river banks
The brooding tripe in a castaway mood
The icons of dark thoroughfares
All refuse burial in the evil forest.

Dispel the morbid solicitude in the waterways
The unwanted company in a festive orchestra,
Winsome and conventional, and the cannonade
Of dumb choirmasters in the cathedral

Clogging the road to eternal light
On the haunches of a twisted foliage
The aftertaste posts pitfalls and daggers
The festering barbarity on the archways.

II
Daylight hides a cluster of loathers
The wreckers of white pianos
Necks heavy with barrels of oil
The green leafage feeds on ash and salt

They are the freaks of the frontier
The owners of standing-on-the-head wisdom
Eyes reddish and twitching
With frothing day- break palm wine
And supple entrails of a goat.

Harbingers of scarlet perspectives, throbbing in the air
The mellifluous dissonance loud in overcast skies
Festering the interstices with resonant calm
Focused, like a wall gecko following a target

Suckled by their pulses and inner voices
Impure as adulterated dewdrops; the full pouch
Shrinks in bad weather –
The ladder is nothing without its rungs...

III
The rainbow shrinks in her lofty home
And green goes on French leave
The colour of drought and stench
Takes over improvident streams and canals
Authors of the stillness of the universe.

The unseen claws, primordial spleen;
The blossom of the rose
Meets a foil in a depraved soul
A blot on the white garment
Of the guardian angel.

Light grieves disconsolately
In the patrimony
Of saltless breath, scourges
The surge of supple chapels
Underground powerhouses and tepid hymnals.

A LAYMAN'S VOCATION

I
The waves are high
And sulphuric and interminable
They pummel the tidy judgment of things
The nude outposts on the shores
Heaping slurs on the mind of God.

The saint smokes out His brain and baggage
Held up in simulates
Like rabbits at Ogwashi-Uku
Lapsing into coma, the starlight,
Hysterical but circumspect, swaps

The frozen underbrush
Of bones and quicksilver
For butterflies, languishing on rooftops
Fates laborious and precipitate
The primitive affinities of man.

The looting bond, volley of sensual blood
The privation under the bush mango tree
 In full season at twilight;
The breeze cool and redolent,
Like the unflapping hovering
Of a thousand pigeons.

II
The destitution in the cathedral
Unveils the bonfire of wrecked souls
Gathering thorns for a garden in heaven
Hedged by a banner of colourful cloths.

The trappings of a synthetic spirit,
Dour and ponderous,
Without stitches or plasters on the navel
In the rebounding darkness.

The haunches and vacuities
Sweating chattels devoid of flames
Transcendental in their underground blaze
The terrestrial lightning in the wilderness

A clatter of bones, grazing without blood
In gusts of empty wind
Shutting down iron doors
On pistols in their cordage

The pile of sins growing by the second
 Drowned in the sanctified appellations
Adorning the stony heritage
In a whorl of light

The infinite crumbs in the sky
Like drapery; let the music
Bleed away boulders of the soul
The burst of shrieking owls.

LIKE A NEWBORN DOG

These honeycombs are burnished
With genitals of songsters
Supple and poppy, like a newborn dog.

They are the bugles of blood moons
Squall of improvident beggars
The circumlocutions of a cosy catechist.

Whoever restores the slashed honey on the altar
Compounds the cobble and dead ends
No one talks of seedlings
Or eyeballs or high hips

In a metallurgical factory –
A flowering oesophagus hides in the dark
Pulsed in serpentine halo
Crackling the compliments

They flounder in their heroic satiny
Or contrived godliness during communion
 The phosphor of secret ravishment
Or quotidian settings beyond poetry's voice!

The confraternity of the empty wind
The incorrigible obfuscation of things and spheres
Ribbons of fire tumble from the twin towers
Dispel the robes of dust and bleach.

II

Whistles do not tell the whole truth
From North to South;
East to West
In a patched union; too much geometry
Of tribe or clique or drossy blood

The ruin of reason and song
The dour foliage of a garden
By living waters oblivious
Of the broken tide

The ditty roar of the ocean at Agge
Its cadences can overtake the world –
The threshed oil- slick poisons the plumage
The defilades far ahead in the race

Showing off their oft underprized flair
Drilled deep into our being
The heartbeat of dust
In gloom or light or the tale in-between.

ASCENTS AND SLASHES

Sometimes, our dreams
Summon us to jarred blossoms
Summon us to ascents and slashes
After all, nobody owns the universe
And its crowded shadows

In the ash and green of spheres
The undulating waves at twilight
 In the constant migration
To all sorts of places in the air
Goaded on by the lyrics' alluring essence.

Flowers sprout on a dead stump
 The hoarded sizzle is a waste
Like inedible fish, their lives or value
Snuffed out by oil- slick or greasy tide.

Nothing stays forever on rooftops
 When volcanoes can fix a fate
In a split second
Without compunction or circumspection

When the gushing semen dries up
On the way to the womb
Missing the drowning carnival of blood
 On Mount Everest in the Far East.

II
Hunt down the cannons from the valley
 Pin them to clogged circles
Furtive essences, full of false flutes
Blowing away the fortune in the wind.

Harden the meadows, or is it hysterical?
Let them spurt shadows and stones
Defying inquisition or Audu's* frog jump –
A colossal shift from the centring waterspout.

This crap of pitiless jars on the soul
Lengthening the threadbare essence
Of dungeons in free climes
The regimentals of freezes in full bloom
When the sun goes down; that impulse

To roof a house without a foundation
Simply intriguing, but
The fragile stairways make circumspection useless
A bonfire marks luminous breaches
On the runway to nirvana

The absorbing red portals
On the Internet
Rotund smell of sulphur and lemonade
Dressed in multiple colours
Like a monarch butterfly

Sheer fathoms of roses
Darken the assemblies of men

Shivering in their brainwaves –
A menacing memory singes itself
On a platter of harrows, without faltering
This is no abstract thing
Or something sundered before breath.

---

* A soldier attached to Government College Bomadi in the seventies andeighties
   to instildiscipline

BLACK TWERKING

The wind itself is bruised on the back
 In the harmattan, in its heaving span
Encloses a verdure sweetness
As fleeting as a toddler's mood
Giving the destitute a rung of hope

In the early morning dew
 In wild forests
A fatuous omelette and bonfire
In the neighbourhood, the sticky gravitas
In the secret smoke and gunpowder of saints

In the free-wheeling sucking
Of the red chambers
Propping up lateral stripes, trills of epic feats
Black twerking, juddering inside the thicket.

A leaking mote endangers the rivers
A buzzing corpse, threshed out of inheritance
There is no expendable blood
In human hierarchies.

Nocturnes takeover the galleries
In broad daylight, multiply the aromatic
Nothing falters in a dance of nakedness
Pummelled by opium or roving pebbles

And the dry effluvium of the masses
The loaded phosphor peddled with piety
The abiding unction and drought
Nourishing terrestrial hips and tombs.

II

Survival is a weak student;
Learns nothing of harmattan or waterfalls
Dissolves in its own pressure
Unscathed in its endless apotheosis

Full of sand and water, hedged in space
The exhaustive rumination in a world
Without alphabet; constellations litter the gutter

Full of stones and strife
In ways providence holds in awe.
The ravishment floats always
An unfailing pollutant like oil-slick in Ezetu[*]

This paradise of feathers
The wasted salt piling up on the planet
Serpents' insignia of dominion or pageantry
The equivocal whirlwinds and estrangement.

---

[*] A town in Southern Ijaw, Bayelsa State, Nigeria.

NO HECKLES IN THE SOUL OF A SAINT

I
Celebrate the triumph in obstinate waters
The plentitude in weevil and drought
There is no sterility in heaven
In the vastness of the spirit.

The ditches gulp the muddy gale
From the deepest bedrooms in the sky
The jamboree and ultimate footfalls
Drenched in Sacristies; the unflagging

Causeways and lodestones in tow
Petals grow pensive in the deepest valleys
Fetid shawls lacking upbraiding
Flaunting casseroles

The guilt in the air rejects penitence
 In a one- way passion
Like a dynamite in the river
It sees no heckles in the soul

The spirited towering of smoke
Written in vagrant scripts
Peddled by mouths slack in profile
Heaping damnation on the godhead

The smouldering company of threshers
Who see no heckles in the spider's web
Supplements can purify stones
In sunburst solicitude and spells

The chick that was hatched
In the rainy season
May not understand
The power of the hawk.

II
The earthly saint is a consummate smoker –
In the wind; his counterpart
Is nightfall in aphrodisiacal dance steps
Both paddle on free land to their prisons In the sky.

There is no fracture
In a squadron worth its salt
No blossom parades irregular greens
No government glows on grinding horsetails
Abiding lanterns in the village square

No manna in rinces and reservoirs
The mesh of faces ends up
In tumid haunches
Without armour or plumage, a postulant
Vocation with fangs for entertainment

Green workmen who bestride gullies
 Remain anonymous, by default;
They are a brimming marmalade marking
The resurrection and song.

A MUDDY GALE

The shattered beginnings and pontifical slips
Breaking bonds of daylight
Only thrive as a whisper
Like the muddy gale which hit a woman's breast
Unseen, after a ditty quarrel with her house help.

What does the seer in the sun say?

It's from an ancestral forest
 Holding up a genealogy
In the middle of a Delta village.

A gargantuan nothing? Soils its heavenly claims?

Nothing is expendable in a world where
A dove's shadow hovers over a flowing stream
 And the encircling vegetation withers

Or a neighbour greets a couple
Set for a fishing expedition
And they return with an empty canoe

Or a sage stares at a thriving store
In the village early in the morning
And the whole day passes by
Without a single sale.

The world cruises on a fragile causeway
 Impervious to scarab whims

The importunate pebbles on the seashore,
 Pensive and luminous
Know not their fate with the tide
A bloom signals terrestrial strength
A greenery of implacable furrows?

II
The leper has a place in heaven
Unless a monstrous cadaver in spirit
Supine in the skein of silvery flakes
Without blots or, rather, with invisible blots

On the sweetness of sea breeze
Plunged in acidulous bubbles
Like soft newborns drenched
In black waters
Of raffia palm groves at Torugbene.

III
The moonlight exudes a surreal freshness
Over the village cathedral
A sweet sparkle in the wilderness
Boundless as life.

A surfeit of lemon draws tears
Drilled into the fading light
At sunset, the wind rocking the shield
The skirmish real and heckling

As a bone of tilapia stuck in the throat
As implacable as a chasing swarm of bees
At Agbayabou,* a mournful whiteness

---

* A mystical forest in Ndoro, Bayelsa State.

Heralds headlands in the wilderness
 Acting the spoiler in the wind
Sundered blood irrigates stones
Brings man back to earth
In soldered songs carrying water.

A FLAILING HIBISCUS AT TWILIGHT

A weft of airs hides their signature
 A lonely bare- faced seediness
A contrived lodestone in a gust of dust
Smothering claws of antagonists

In an underground blaze; the outer purity is vain
Prefigures a bludgeon of boulders
The unperishable investiture of black labels
The fleeting gloss when the sun
Romances the sea-waves, like a toddler's moods.

The flailing hibiscus at twilight
Threshed in abiding causeways;
Languid cauliflowers, painted on facades
The leprous roots of flower and light

Drilled in time's punctual prompting
Of furrows and drenched spirits;
Adamant gusts of wind
Slashing the sand's surface.

There is a crown of blossoms
 And the leviathan fruits,
Triggering migrations
Across borders, ending up as servants
With no open tunnel; No bastion

To peer into the future,
Bare or husky or boring
A hopeless miasma of prodigal haunches
 Trawlers prey on nothing,
The rivers nuzzled at source.

There is a twilight radiating
The soul of black liquor
A pile of lust on lust on lust–
The wanton delectation of sly souls

A torpid whorl of funeral vocations
The briny latchets, the numbers awful,
The blossoming flower succumbs
To the treachery of the sun

Languid doorways, opened by stench
Bolting perfidy, throbbing in the alleyway
Tickling facades, landing a sullen kiss
On her cheeks, the fecund goddess of strides

Through darkly waters, in smelly cadences
In the quietness of a harmattan morning
On the runway of blood–
A broken staircase to heaven.

THE DEVIL'S ACCENT

They hold up a bag of pomegranate
Bulging in terrestrial light
Goaded on by the silvery accent
Stooges enjoy, on windshield and lightning.

There is a surfeit of waves
On the haunches of muddy air
The harpoon keeps the tribe afloat
Even with fragile lanterns.

Medals always pile up in the wind
 In the jungle of black parrots
Silence gathers no strength
And the multiple migrations across ideologies (if any)
Observe no rules.

In the wilderness
The milkless breast has no pity
O the barbarity of stones and the human heart
Their gaze, though seemingly blank,

Like the newborn's,
Is always on bonfires and banquets
The bland mind's underground gatherings
Tossing naked caprices in the sun

Like a two-year-old's longings in empty space
No one fathoms the joys of pious light
In a fly-infested public toilet
At Burutu waterside.

II
Cannons do not crave compunctions
 In terrestrial spheres
In a plot of invisible padlock;
In their blaze, spirits can live
Both on land and on water

Brook no hiding
In their ambiguous vehemence
Ungraspable through and through
Like the slovenly flowering of seeds
On a garbage dump.

In the (abiding) charm of the chosen ones –
 Every season is harvest time –
The uncountable carnival boats (lining the river)
The unfading crackle
Of crickets and sunbirds

Signal deserted stairways in heaven
The lame trudge at sunlight
In the haloes of hope, crossing
Barriers and harrows in the clouds

The calamity of a motionless forward march
A leprous passion in the moment of reckoning
No pollen in the penthouse
No granary in feet hurrying to perdition.

BARRICADES IN THE STABLE

A verdure of bubbles, wrenched
From a gimcrack graveyard –
The bastion of a million fates
Flowers in the setting sun.

This earth is encumbered
By the pith of patriots-
Fabrications and footnotes
The fleecy gallop of illusions
The encircling pitfalls in moonlight

Punctual, like Victory's* cry
When scolded.

The supreme vehemence of power
The ever- bloating placements
The cannonade of weevils
Living in the bustling streets

The quintessence of dominion over flesh
Blackening the rain on cocoyam leaves
On the seashore and dunghills
Where the somnambulist passes urine

The pimps on midnight dews
On carked vegetation and verdure
No whinnying in songful syllables
Laden with wisecracks and worldly gratuity

---

* Poet's two-and-a-half-years old daughter

A warehouse of glitches and trumpery
Pointing to the weird intestine in the wind
Bile and blighting sickness
In the tusk of the midday sun.

THOSE MAUDLIN MOMENTS

We pluck from the air riddled with roses
Those maudlin moments laid out
In the mind– the ring of dreams
Basking in fair-skinned shadows

Over the merchandise on high seas
The stargazers switch off their trade
Waving off the dark signs assail

It's time we ordered the rainbow
Out of the sky; straws and strictures
Have taken over...

O let the garrisons absorb the light
Bursting beyond the frame
Of a million catechists' glasses.

II
The gravediggers converse in caverns
 A credulous symmetry of ideas
Fresh from the mind's forge

Where necromancers, miserly in their outlook,
Eavesdrop the husks flying loosely
In the wind, in deference
To the lean image in the looking-glass.

Whoever courts bedlam with a sane mind
Even in half- sleep, drained of all splinters
Of emotion, though shimmering in their nudity?

A disheartening lexicon, like mucored bread,
Rubble litters the churches in the neighbourhood
Of disparate origins, all connected
In the spirit of sorcery and sin

Hovering in the dark waters beneath
Haggard homes, without inheritance or heritage,
Playing host to flow stations
Nibbling at their farms and fortune

Where vicars live in bridles
Stalled in their visions
Counterfeit kindred as altar servers
Plundering the dream and pomegranate

Like a swarm of Boko Haram soldiers
Acting on an impulse of lackeys,
Scrappy in disposition, who labour to live
In swathes of meandering heights.

Compradors keep watch over their heads
Without opium or armament
The forbearance itself juicy and mordant
At the same time

In the march beyond bloodlines
Beyond spirited pursuers
Dressed in robes glacial and garish
 And gibberish, gnawing at their souls.

THOSE JUBILANT DARK STARS

Somewhat smug for a star,
Resolute, without effacement, in the inner self,
Smarting from street corner conversations
In the middle of Pentecost.

Tongues wag without end in the wind
 Knock on earth bones and blood
Lacking stamina or moist or swag

They are a bit restless
But integral and unvarying
Throwing off positive extremes
Yet sparkling amongst the countless dark angels

Abettors all, certainly no synonyms
For the scrap wood on show glass in the continent
Like dark smoke curling from a cathedral
Surrounded by a garden of white lilies.

No respite in beautiful geraniums-
The quiet of the ailed or ailing
The unuttered schism in the soul-
No music can ever reach its widest circumference.

All around bathed in carbonized calm
A tremulous broil, without substance
Or serenading stuff;
Just pulling down the garrisons of the wind

The rubble climbs the ladder
To a vacuous plenitude and applause;
A punctual anomaly inhabits the earth
Abhorring sacrifice or prophecy

Or the anguished roar
 Of the lion of Judah
Or the shimmering crackle of the cuckoo
Or the animated pigeons spread out

In the sky, trampling
On flowery yokes and wood smoke
Growing in the mouth of messiahs
Drifts in the monastical underbrush.

THIS EARTH IS A CANVAS

The earth absorbs every image
Nestling in nests and crannogs
Even the credulous cinema of undercurrents
The catechist throws up in the cathedral.

Dressed in baits of patriots
Who distort the symmetry of the sea breeze
Trample the course of galloping antelopes
Glowing in the itinerant puddle.

Beneficent sorcerers, the carking bustle
Of triumphant souls heard in sky-tide
The lingering glitch in the air
Rings like a million church bells

The convergence of carked blood
Without boundary, or frontier; irrepressible
In its violet course, a naked eucalyptus
Carried by the flood as flotsam.

The devil perspires in the anus
Yet carries a rainbow impulse
Illusion lives in supple bridles that abide
In the spirit all around-

Heavy and choking and unyielding
Openly empty of milk
A consummate lackey of banal minds
A dissolute smog hanging in the sky

Full of stamina, the massive claim
Of sunflowers in the desert;
Tangible in the arid air
Creatures savour mileages

In stupor, even without alcohol
Immobile, robotic, the forbearance
Of a born nanny from the South- South
A drained disposition in another world –
 Like white cassava flakes

A nutriment of kindred spirits
Spreading burnished shadows, swathed
In mournful discretions, contaminants
Of that foamy pool of power

Parading a vile latitude, like a boa
Coiled to strike; unvarying in their dark pose
A maniac exploring the bounties of a whore
 Who offers to taste the despoiled earth

In a blind passion, breaking
The crackling shell of vanity Heard In the soul, like music
From the depths of river Forcados

Only *Olorogun* hears; basking
In the wild extremes of creation
The whinnying abuse
Of unmerited inheritance.

Whoever sweats in a sea-ride
In a dank broad daylight,
Without encountering

A wry-smiling mami-wata[*]
Swims in a devious kind of fear,
Bordering on guilt.

---

* Mermaid

THIS AIR IS NOT PURE

This air is not pure
A cyclopean flow in barren skies
Laden with lust; earthy and tinsel,
Seekers of soft spots abound in the sky
Entrenched on our palms!

Born predators of bone and all
Like cats laying claim
To everything in a cat's stomach
Stars of impurities, they
Even pilfer the free air

Never tired of pushing non-initiates
To the periphery of proletarian calculus
A dissolute sorcery to say hell is white.

The signs are always there,
Coalescing, howling within,
Always there for the blind to see (and act on) –
The cripple never dies a known death

Even in craggy corners, withering epochs
Sifting stones from pure breath,
A distillation of raw things
Light up the road to a megalith.

II
The flood lapses right on their lap
An arid concert of galaxies
A lateral dispensation of wantonness
An offlandish posture at their niggardly best.

The heft is a push forward,
Eclipses past heights,
A retrospective pullulating
Bearing the inexorable weight of faltering.

Dusty thoroughfares keeping vigil
Over a spattered lot, engulfing
The madrigal and acidic; soiling playgrounds,
As frustrating as attending to crying twins
At the same time.

The gawky presence of jingoists
And lyricists who smoke weed
To fire their fates to Fahrenheit.

The sizzling slips
Of a soaring incubus
Soulfully blowing undying
Whistles of love

As *Olorogun* is urged on
In its dire mission
By the sound of its cognomen:
Ala beni kolokolo.[*]

Disheartening drifts in full cycle
Beget a naked hole in the cathedral
 Like thunder or an explosion
Unsettling white pigeons in the air.

---

[*] *Olorogun*'s appellation.

WHINNYING WITH BROOMS

A beneficent curse;
A firebrand drowsiness
Before the heat of mangrove fire;
There is no point whinnying with brooms

Over crooked paths
In a show of symmetry across borders.

The coffin-maker jubilates over more work
In the air; a counterfeit credulity
In the spirit, a lackey passion
Bereft of blood, a seedy gravitas.

Illusion evolves from the trenches
Spread out in battlefields of the soul
 Drained of every integral good thing
 Like an unbridled mad cow

Trampling on the genuine impulse
Of the Samaritan, lachrymose
Like an unfailing traitor;
Or the fate

Of a native fowl
That likes to play
In a native doctor's compound

An unvarying shadow of things
Pervades the air

Lurking like the morning star
Milky in its misleading sparkle
The patriot primed with inner guilt
 Is crestfallen at the freshness
Of garbage-dump cocoyam

The true catechist is unfouled
By masqueraders in the cathedral;
The rainbow cancels out
Lapsing stars in the sky.

An odorous moonlit field in eventide
 Expansive in its disheartening lure;
Dissolute lackeys swathed
In the pangs of unremembering

Punctual in their dragnets
Mournful exploits of undertakers
The anomalous passion
Of the earless housefly!

A taste of converse niceties
In their hoarse voices, absorbing
The distorted air and rubble
The rainbow embodies
A carking army of deference

The throng too happy to feast
On the dour inheritance
They spread their jokers in secret
In the pure potentials of pen and paper.

HOMEWARD BOUND

Beyond bridle and barricade
A maudlin choice is made
Between the chimeras
And the dour corners of the earth.

The husks of high taste
In the season of Pentecost
Open cornets, sundering thrushes
Broken wings, bewitched lustre

The odour of armpits and janjaweed
The smog prophecies of butter and bread
The inner propulsion of a singing bird
Prowling through scrap wood

Sonorous and nutritious
A rainbow disrupts endearment
Even in self-effacement, with loud eyelashes
The milky measure of a sunbeam

In all its fleeting grandeur
Silent and flaming, like mangrove wood fire
The barrels of crude drained
By drift or graft
Nebulous in the nourishment they bring to the soul

Like a hidden gem swathed
In a catechism of fate
Like spectators' chants of "*Asakpiyei eh, Asakpiyei eh.*"*
Urge *Olorogun* not to give up the chase
Sprinting in a punctual tide.

_____

* The *runners'* challenge Olorogun to a sprinting battle.

Always, the earth
Embowels a drowning sparkle
Incandescent clogs shrouded in treachery
Carbonized in the homeward journey
That ends in profound nothing.

II
The trailing shadow keeps us company
Like an impotent powerhouse in the creeks
Now the flood has suspired
In the parched glands of the shore.

Midnight men ring the church bell
Drowning their covert movements
In the graveyard amid
The owl's ceaseless shriek.

Scraps of hell live with us on earth
Overgrown on the gonad of gloom
Throbbing in the green and white
Our flag carries, laden with water and fire.

The phosphorescence of a sea god
In its underwater cavern, basking in song and slip
Both balanced in some ethereal mystic equation
And the moon presages the doomsday

On the arms of a mermaid
Marooned in her own home
Unwilling to give up the bond
In spite of the pressures
Of western theology.

LINES ON OUR PALMS

And a tangible fate devolves
On slaying children,
As crowded as *ozubu* playground
In a masquerade outing; they are swayed

By wayward bubbles beyond blood
Unseen with naked eyes.

A loaded lapidist blows hot
Pulling down pathways paved with flowers
Life's offerings that become bloated
In tunnels, in the assegais of airy flight.

The turbulence is engraved on their palms
Lacks penance; whoever seeks salvation in the grave
Floating among lost souls
On the way to Nirvana!

Whoever suckles the lines on our palms –
Undecipherable in their tell-tale luminosity!
The moon halves the secret chambers
Of a maiden at twilight

The green forests deaf to the sound
Of cajolers who maraud the tombs of damsels
Flower them with mundane earth
Giggling in their closets after upturning

The course of the gods, the drug silting up
Their pistons in the middle of the sea

Is it solitude or stupor
That breeds sterile dreams
Awakens men to black routes
Beside the riverside

The mangrove fire drying up
The tributaries of memory,
Otherwise inextinguishable?

The earth is eloquent in her slimy entrails
Like whining monsters, bringing down rains
In torrents, their tepid eyelids laden with lies

Discreet and crystalline, ruminating on plumes
Of the apocalypse on a god's lap
Forming a parallel government in disguise

On black streets, tiptoeing on the galaxy
Of fables scattered across the moon
Draped in drowsy milt, courting *Owigiri** dancers
Throbbing in their waists (which is the centre of gravity)

Soaked in demagogues' sober speeches;
The bloom and plasma
The good soul is always in labour-
Inner sweat, absorbing multiple malcontents,

The sinew stalls of the sea, slung
By rulers of darkness,
In the quiet nutriment of green.

---

* Ijaw highlife dance

HUMANS

A tangible shadow, like the smog of arson
Ignoring water from body and space
Sometimes, pestilence is the whistle
Of the gods to dreamy humans
To have a bearing in their dizzy convoys
The burst of incandescence in precipitate boulders

Dragging man's ears to a grave point
The carking indifference, the bloated mania
In the looking- glass of towers
The mawky miasma of die-hard clauses

Knotty bougainvillea, feathery endearments
Of the soul, spattered with abandon
In the wind, causing premature wrinkles and stroke
Hafts in the service of mundane canons

Looking down on God's creation
From the mountaintop without a mandate
Abiding manure of affirmations
A perpetual lackey in the desert

The young standing nipples in the dark –
Formations that spawn fabrications
Or expanded truths, crisp bones
Scurrilous homesteads always in moonlight

Pure, like pristine poetry in wood smoke
The monotonous strides of a bewitched wayfarer
Boulders of carbonized pubescence, sundered sizzle
Catlike footfalls of seducers, without lustre

Like lofty destinies detained in coven
Making a fossil of hackles in open legs
Motes forever recondite and recalcitrant
Crestfallen before the burden or lance-point

Falling headlong into the abyss
The tantalizing fruitage on hairy chests
Ambiguous altars, always holding sway
Which is a dark omen

Altogether transcendental in their hilly solicitude
In the aromatic leprosy in the city
Needless to talk about despoiled saints
Always in stupor, in bonfires water cannot quench.

The heated arguments serve well
Like a cumulus spread out in the sun
The shuddering grief, prophetical anomalies
Expansive intonation, bereft of discretion
Like yelling spectators
When *Olorogun* breaks a canoe to pieces.

THE SCARAB SONG
For Hanifa Abubakar*

In view of
The full-throated growl of thunder
In a night when the moon
Smiles through jocund mangrove groves

Purify the soul of the earth.

The bare-faced masquerades
Pursuing us in our dreams
The despoiled cradles
Dandling oozing carrions,

Purify the soul of the earth

The world whirls at the fumes
Flowing from holy altars
The crackle of broken bedrooms
Riddled with impotent grey –

Spoiling the sunny spell in the tunnel
That generates its own juice
A songful repository
Arching on fallen walls –

Pigs in Christmas robes
Crisp and sexy, stalking
The alligator in its fluvial house
The illusion of mourning

---

* A five-year-old kid who was poisoned to death and buried in Kano State, Nigeria by
  abductors led by her teacher

Grave clothes and painted lips
Laying wreaths in the wind.

Purify the soul of the earth

II
Living apertures augment the false plumage
The lament from canals and cathedrals
The flailing fathoms of merchandise
The muddling of salt by postmen on rampage

A damsel foils romance in the sun
Seeking renewal in ritual and liturgy
The rather extortionate tastes of our sons
In nameless entanglements overseas

On the World Wide Web

Wearing high heels
To pack palm kernels
From racks beyond reach

Oiling the enterprise
With mortal blood
And muddled mumbling

Purify the soul of the earth

See the drove in the dark
Sluicing in sin
The Chrisland stench**
Only a tip.
Canons take the back seat
On the decibel of graven things

** The viral sex video of a ten-year-old female student of Chrisland Schools, Lagos

The mind is a malleable place
In labyrinthine spheres;
A slate for the gods' algorithms

The poet's tongue
Is a book of psalms
Littered with scars

Reminder of the bruises
Of too much talking
To thunderstorms at twilight

Purify the soul of the earth.

O what does one say
Of the Kano rabbi
Who poisoned his own pupil -

The radiant preschooler-
And buried her parts
Right in the premises

Yanking out dream
From tender loins
Into eternal lake of dream
In the frowning moonlight?

A weird kind of nakedness
You can say again and again -
The phosphorous breath -
Licensed and licentious,
The onlooker stupefied
By the ambiguity

And portentousness

The rapacious pitfalls, the empty vociferation
The booty of perfidy swelling by the day –
A kind of freedom laden with fever
In festering black waters

Where children take their spirit –
Gaunt and oozing in blood and bone
Harried and extravagant
Ravishers of hallowed domains

Tart to underground deals, whispering
Lightning strides in the cove –
A perfumed serpent –
Vehement and unforgiving

They are the shadows of meadows
And dewy doorways
The smouldering lords of the wind
The venomous supplicant in holy altars

The improvident stalkers
 Of voice and ware dappled.

Purify the soul of the earth

So we can wash our heads
at the waterfront with *ẹgịran asọn*^{***}
And sing the scarab song
In the unfurling sun.

*** A kind of native soap. The usage here is actually an adaptation of the Izon
   saying

Purify the soul of the earth.

Printed in the United States
by Baker & Taylor Publisher Services